Th… de l'Orangerie

PIERRE GEORGEL

Translated from the French
by John Adamson

GALLIMARD
RÉUNION DES MUSÉES NATIONAUX

Claude Monet, *Les Tuileries, étude*, 1875, Musée d'Orsay, Paris

journey and made to feel the idea of the infinite. The strict east-west orientation – the historic axis of Paris, along which the Tuileries Gardens are aligned – coincides with the sun's apparent trajectory, a supreme instance of cosmic order exalted by the *Water-lilies*. It was not long before they too unashamedly followed suit, for at the east end were clustered the morning compositions with their willows and at the other the dazzling spectacle of the sunset. The very seclusion of the 'waterside' terrace and the contrast with the hubbub of the Place de la Concorde were also contributory factors. It was as if the building were destined to become, in keeping with the declared aim of the artist, a haven for modern man with his 'strained nerves', who would come there to reflect and be reinvigorated. Lastly, the landscapes to the north and south were none other than some of Monet's favourite views transformed into his pictorial legacy: the garden, nature in miniature – from the Tuileries of his youth to the lyrical microcosm of Giverny – and the Seine, a waterscape he held dear all his life.

Of the sacred and the profane

The identity of the Orangerie (now with a capital O) was to be altered forever by this intimate accord – sealed with a sacred seal – between the aim of the *Water-lilies* and the casket chosen to

In memory of Jean Lebrat,
recalling our steep climb.

'The only one of its kind'

Here is a glimpse of the waxing and waning fortunes of the stone shell built at the bottom of the Tuileries Gardens under Napoleon III. Starting life as an orangery, it became a museum at first only housing the *Water-lilies*, later achieving the splendid and memorable twofold function it has today. The museum is 'the only one of its kind', to quote the prophetic tribute made by six eminent intellectuals campaigning to save it and published in *Le Monde*. What makes the museum so unique has still not been fully appreciated; here we attempt to find out what that is.

The *Water-lilies* and the genius loci

When on 6 April 1921 Claude Monet chose the converted orangery to accommodate what he called his 'great work' (to which he had devoted the previous seven years, and before that almost twenty mulling the idea over), he had already considered and discarded several sites. Notable among these was the main courtyard of the brand new Rodin museum, installed in a fine 18th-century townhouse. Following a disagreement with the architect, that project was abandoned, but the real issue lay in the fact that Monet had no key reason for opting for that location. That things turned out so differently for the Orangerie is in part owing to circumstances. The building, which Monet adopted after a little demur, had not been long in the hands of the Administration des Beaux-Arts and happened to be available, and Clemenceau, his old crony but also the influential statesman, had the bright idea to suggest it. Yet circumstances alone would not have sufficed. What really justified his choice was the fact that the creator of the *Water-lilies* perceived a consonance between the genius loci and the intention of the work itself. It enabled him to advance towards accomplishing his aims.

There were so many things about these gardens on the banks of this river that struck the right chord. The oblong shape of the orangery lent itself better than any other to creating the effect of 'everything without end' that Monet had had in contemplation for nearly twenty-five years. He still only had an inchoate notion of a circular panorama around a central vantage point. But once the location had been secured, his plan shifted from circle to oval, and on to a double ellipse set lengthways so that visitors were led on a truly endless working for so long in the privacy of his prolific retreat. But the methods were quite different. Like the *Water-lilies*, the Paul Guillaume Collection was the product of supreme individuality manifesting itself as much in its general arrangement as in the choice of each painting. At the same time, it was the backdrop to a message to the public, albeit a smaller audience than that for the *Water-lilies*. For if Monet opened his 'haven' to a vast uprooted humanity, Paul was only minded to woo a public with a potential interest in modern art. A few decades later, by a stroke of good fortune, these two autonomous yet strangely matching creations were brought together within the walls of the Orangerie; the first the work of one of the greatest artists there has ever been, the second that of an art lover of the first water, both merely following their ideals and both resolved to share them.

Paul Guillaume congratulated himself on having brought together 'the most complete and dazzling representation in the world, after the Barnes Foundation ..., of French painting of the last fifty years'. That was something of an overstatement and the critic Waldemar George was nearer the mark when he proclaimed a museum 'incomplete perhaps but containing the essentials and subject to expansion'. Other than the fact that it only concerned itself with French art (but included great immigrant figures of the 'School of Paris'), the collection was limited to what constituted the known territory of 'living art', from Impressionism to Cubism and its immediate successors, and ignored later avant-garde artists. Moreover, within these parameters, the list of absentees was endless. Only Cézanne and Renoir represented Impressionism; there were no Gauguins, no van Goghs, no Nabis or Fauves, and Matisse and Derain were only represented by their later paintings. Among the Cubists, there was neither Braque nor Léger, the latter admittedly nearer to the purist and abstract avant-garde than to the Cubism of before 1914. That said, few modern art collections of the inter-war years could boast of such a concentration of high-quality works. In 1927 Waldemar George estimated the collection, on top of a considerable assemblage of 'African' sculptures, at 'five hundred paintings, among them top-ranking pieces by Renoir, Picasso and Rousseau' – to which he might have added Cézanne, Derain, Matisse, Utrillo, Soutine and Modigliani in particular. The collection caused quite a stir when about a third was put on show two years later in an exhibition which the leading art journal *Cahiers d'art* hailed as 'the best group of contemporary paintings ever shown in Paris'. With such a sizeable asset, Paul could quietly flaunt his belief in modern art in the face of philistines and intellectuals of any hue or colour.

Yet by then a new front line was being drawn. Since the last war years an unprecedented clash had arisen within the ranks of modern art itself, signalling a rift between the old and new members of the avant-garde; the first (let us say, those of the Apollinaire school) borne along by a humanist purpose even in their onslaughts on the house this treasure. The refurbishment of the interior, clearly inspired by religious architecture (the enclosed structure of the two great rooms, the lobby serving as a *pronaos* to a temple of art) was soon to endorse and reinforce this identity.

The opening in 1927 of the 'Claude Monet museum' in the half of the building allotted to the *Water-lilies* raised the question about the appropriateness of the word 'museum' – a label applied no doubt purely out of administrative routine. No heed was paid to the fact that the idea of art as a means of transcendence in succession to religion was intrinsic to the original concept of a museum. The Third Republic's educational doctrine assigned a totally different mission, turning the museum first and foremost into an instrument of 'public edification', whereas the *Water-lilies* were precisely the negation of this system. As a poem to the infinite and (to stay with Monet's own terms) an invitation to 'peaceful meditation', the paintings do not impart any specific learning; instead they give rise to reverie rather than to reflexion and elude discursive commentary. Clemenceau had encountered this intangibility. Wishing to compile, like some grand old man of the Enlightenment, a visitor's explanatory 'guide', he soon discovered that it was no easy task!

Yet in spite of this incongruity, the Administration des Beaux-Arts carried on regardless. In the unoccupied space at the Orangerie it set up a busy exhibition gallery and launched a programme along its own lines. So there was contemplation, stillness, timelessness on one side and thirst for knowledge and bustle of current events on the other. The museum had been reduced to two separate halves sharing the same space, each with its own entrance, and this odd yoking together was bound to mar the identity stamped on the place by the *Water-lilies*. True, they were then totally out of vogue, and until the 1960s when abstraction afforded them a fresh look, the public only really went to the Orangerie to see the random succession of exhibitions held there as if it was a venue of little consequence.

A grand scheme

In 1927, the very year that the orangery-turned-museum began its new lease of life, the press announced the imminent opening of the 'first French museum of modern art'. It was revealed that, contrary to expectation, this new museum would not be state run, but was the brainchild of a private individual, the picture dealer Paul Guillaume, at that time one of the celebrities of Paris cultural life. His superb private collection that he and a few other privileged individuals enjoyed in the graceful interior in which he had lovingly installed it was thus to go public, as were his highly personal views of which it was the inspired expression.

It was rather like the way Monet had made available to the public, in the institutional context of a museum, the work of art on which he had been

Wallace Collection in London or the Musée Jacquemart-André in Paris), containing no other collection but his own presented, moreover, exactly as it was originally. In short, this was the exact opposite of the pattern in regular public museums, where acquisitions from a miscellany of sources are clustered together in a group that imposes its own meaning, one which is doomed to espouse the norms of the majority. The conviction behind this solution was readily apparent, whatever other motivations there might have been. Fulfilling an outstanding mission of service to the public, in this instance affirming the grandeur of modern art and letting the masses enjoy it, was best not left to the State, inherently condemned to conformism. Independence of thought, underpinned by total commitment, would do a better job per se: hence the twin concerns of making the collection accessible and preserving its unique flavour by giving the trivialities and incongruities of a 'real' museum a wide berth.

Paul Guillaume's widow and heir, Domenica Walter, endeavoured to achieve this in her turn. Having taken over from her husband (who in the meantime had forsaken the idea of a private museum) the mission to bring his grand scheme to fruition, she was to come to an agreement with the Administration to install the collection at the Orangerie in the temporary exhibition space: the scale of the museum, akin to that of a big private dwelling, ensured that Paul's collection would be housed there intact, its only company being the *Water-lilies*.

Rethinking a museum

Thus it was that a second extraordinary 'discourse' had just joined Monet's, or better still, a second 'poem' invested with the same aura of freedom and intimacy. Yet these two ensembles remained very different in character, and there was also the problem of the separate and highly disparate scheduling for the exhibition gallery. Would the architectural restructuring necessitated by the arrival of the collection at last provoke discussion at State level? Could the terms of this trinomial be coordinated and attuned to the genius loci?

Nothing of the sort: although the building underwent lengthy reconstruction (1960-65), there was no overall plan. The only guideline given to the architect was to house the collection willy-nilly, within spaces redolent of a private dwelling but nevertheless functioning as a museum. This was accomplished to the detriment of the *Water-lilies*. Their magisterial setting was devastated and they were cut off from daylight by a concrete slab. They were relegated to a backwater and subordinated to the flow of the collection. And as this collection had been bequeathed with the proviso under the terms of a usufruct that it would remain at Domenica's home until her death, the space earmarked for it was in the interim allocated to temporary exhibitions, which succeeded one another without rhyme or reason. The Orangerie remained a clutch of locations, of collections – if the *Water-lilies* can really be called a 'collection' – and of aims rubbing past, the second (Dada, the Surrealists) rejecting pell-mell the values of the past and present. This was aggravated by the multifaceted 'return to order' of the 1920s, where a nostalgia for repressed values (order, tradition, beauty) blended with the demoralizing effect of the war and the political conservatism of the time. It marked a shift away from the innovative drive at the dawning of the century and even appeared retrograde. In the eyes of the custodians of the modernist flame, Picasso painting subjects from Antiquity or Matisse depicting odalisques and Nice interiors constituted reprehensible acts of betrayal.

But nothing was more foreign to Paul Guillaume, a historical modernist, than modernist dogmatism. In that regard he ended up abiding by the lessons of Apollinaire, who had been his mentor in his early years and in whom the taste for adventure and true support for dissidents went hand in hand with real intellectual liberalism. Just as Apollinaire was able to applaud the apparent volte-face of a Derain – from his 'barbarous juvenilia' to an utterly classical measure – so our dealer-collector was able to go beyond purely theoretical contradictions. On his walls the 'negro' Picasso, the Cubist canonized by modernist doctrine, hung alongside the 'neo-classical' Picasso – albeit bearing the indelible stamp of the Cubist experiment – rejected by the intransigent 'moderns'. Then again there was the quasi-abstraction of Matisse's *Leçon de piano* and the subtle melding of reality and abstraction in Soutine and Modigliani. To both those opposed to modern art and radical fanatics, the collection responded with a concentration of masterpieces whose splendour was self-evident and where tradition alternated with modernity or merged with it.

Adopting stances

Paul was thus not alone in believing in the timeliness of giving Paris a modern art museum worthy of the name. In intellectual circles, they were vying with each other to denounce the bureaucratic machine of the 'Beaux-Arts' – 'those political parasites', as Paul genially dubbed them, 'whom we euphemistically call civil servants'. They took up the cudgels against the inertia of the sad Musée du Luxembourg. This museum had been devoted to the works of 'living artists' for a hundred years, but refused categorically, in compliance with a republican principle of equality, to delineate specifically modern art from within the whole contemporary artistic output. And in rebuttal of this distributive justice, they preached critical discernment, the adopting of a stance, acquiring a taste for enterprise and risk, in other words they professed the dynamism and vigour of imagination found in the private sector. As much an established man of business as a man of taste and culture, Paul endeavoured to be the living illustration of this ultra-liberal thesis.

Of significance here is the formula he conceived for his forthcoming museum: a 'townhouse-museum', in truth more 'townhouse' than 'museum', situated in his own home (like the

freedom and lyricism' that had won the plaudits of *Cahiers d'art*. The assemblage nevertheless remained of outstanding quality, but henceforward favoured the classicizing dimension of modern art, in diametric opposition to current taste. In the revised and amended form in which it came to the Orangerie, the Collection was a bit like a 'salon des refusés' to Beaubourg's Académie.

The *Water-lilies* had been betrayed and sidelined. The Collection, discredited because it was out of step with the times and blunted by a meaningless presentation, was eclipsed by the lavish displays at Beaubourg and the Musée d'Orsay, of which the little Orangerie might at most be said to be the poor cousin. Who would risk gambling on it? Rather than assess its attributes, it was merely kept alive.

Contrary to all expectations

This blinkered view would certainly have persisted if unexpected factors had not intervened.

In the first instance, there was an unprecedented growth in attendance exceeding all forecasts and, since there had been no special publicity campaign, this betokened a self-generated and lasting popularity. There are many reasons underlying this. Some have to do with global growth in cultural consumption; others are linked particularly to the nature of the collections and their greatly renewed significance. The *Water-lilies* had emerged from their limbo, and post-modern sensibility inclined the public to look with new eyes at works of art that modernist orthodoxy had spurned, like those superlatively represented at the Orangerie. No doubt the mammoth scale and encyclopaedic ambition of the 'grands musées' nearby also prompted a reaction in favour of intimacy of scale, focus of thought, primacy of quality and moderation in quantity. That said, the ever-growing numbers of visitors, packed into the cramped 1960s rooms, urgently necessitated a fresh look at the public areas.

Secondly, there was the increasingly glaring dichotomy between the shabby state of the Orangerie and the opulence of its mighty neighbours, especially after the 'Grand Louvre' project got under way at the other end of the gardens. Jean Lebrat, chairman of the public entity entrusted with that colossal undertaking, also pressed hard for a renovation programme for the Orangerie. He was the only one among the 'decision-makers' to deem it both necessary and welcome.

One last factor was the unstinting work of the new museum director, who took up his post in 1993. Without going into the details of the trials and tribulations along the way, suffice it to say here that his efforts would restore both meaning and dignity to the building and its treasures.

The four successive states of the Orangerie:
models made by Artefact, Paris (2006)

shoulders under the same roof. And this state of affairs only grew worse when what was now dubbed the Jean Walter and Paul Guillaume Collection was permanently accessioned in 1984. There was not even enough room to give any information about its history, and the altogether too restrictive pre-ordained plan prevented any internal rejigging. The visitor might well have wondered what all those fine pictures were doing together and why they were there rather than somewhere else. It would all have been somewhat absurd if the curator, Michel Hoog, had not successfully mounted a few good exhibitions tying in with the specific themes of the museum in the remaining space available.

That was not all. Almost sixty years after the 'townhouse' museum had been announced, nobody seemed to have taken on board that the situation that had explained and justified Paul's course of action had altered! The triumph of modern art, in his time still utopian, had been achieved: the 'agents' of change had broken through; cultural democratization and a slow shift of opinion did the rest. The State itself had begun to rally round shortly after Paul's death. Before long it had created the great museum of modern art so desperately awaited, the absence of which Paul had done his utmost to rectify. The moment for his 'first French museum of modern art' had thus passed, and its obvious merit had lost its edge. As a symbol for the efficiency of the 'private' sector over the 'public', the project misfired; as an expression of personal taste, the collection may have seemed arbitrary. True, it retained all its brilliance as testimony to the wonders of modern art, but the old Musée du Luxembourg was no longer there as a foil. Besides which, in the space of a few decades the Administration went from one extreme to the other. It ended up supporting the most reputedly subversive aspects at the heart of modern art, the very same ones that the avant-garde artists of the 1920s had exalted to the exclusion of everything else. Having taken the place of the timorous Luxembourg, the Musée d'Art Moderne was in turn regarded in the 1970s as being too timorous and was absorbed into the ostensibly avant-garde structure of 'Beaubourg' (the Centre Pompidou), which opened not with a Matisse or Picasso exhibition but with one dedicated to the epitome of the anti-artists, Marcel Duchamp. Against this backdrop, the inveterate liberalism of Paul Guillaume, with his notion of great 'French painting' where 'ancient' and 'modern' sat harmoniously side by side, seemed, to say the least, ill-timed!

This is especially true given that the content of the collection itself had undergone notable transformations, which markedly upset its fine balance. Determined to carry on the work of Paul but endowed with a taste that was less assured and daring, Domenica acquired some excellent paintings by Cézanne and Renoir, but sold off many modern paintings. Among those were *Demoiselles à la rivière* and the *Leçon de piano* by Matisse, and most of Picasso's 'negro' and Cubist canvases. These had been the archetypes of the 'spirit of

Exhibition of the Société Centrale d'Horticulture held at the Orangerie des Tuileries in 1878

From orangery to museum

The Musée de l'Orangerie is one of the first examples of a utilitarian building converted into a cultural site. As its name reminds us, it is housed in an old orangery, built at the beginning of the Second Empire on the southern terrace of the Tuileries Gardens. Subsequently put to all manner of uses – army depot, billet for mobilized soldiers, venue for sporting, musical or patriotic spectacles, for horticultural, dog or trade shows – only seldom was it used for artistic events. In 1921, however, the building was allotted a function befitting its imposing architecture. Along with the Jeu de Paume, its symmetrical counterpart across the gardens, it was handed over to the Administration des Beaux-Arts, which planned to turn it into an annexe of the Musée du Luxembourg (forerunner of the Musée National d'Art Moderne). Then at the proposal of his friend Clemenceau, Claude Monet chose it to house his supreme work, the great mural cycle of the *Water-lilies* that he was preparing to donate to the French nation.

Planned in 1850 and, by and large, completed by the architect Firmin Bourgeois two years later in the space of four months, the long rectilinear building has hardly altered on the outside. Its imposing proportions are in keeping with those of the Place de la Concorde, which it overlooks, and much as they were with those of the Tuileries Palace (destroyed long ago), which inspired its east and west fronts, with their sculpted pediments and paired ringed columns. The interior was an empty space, with the north side blind and the south side wholly glazed. It was in this 'loft' before its time that Monet elected to house his *Water-lilies*.

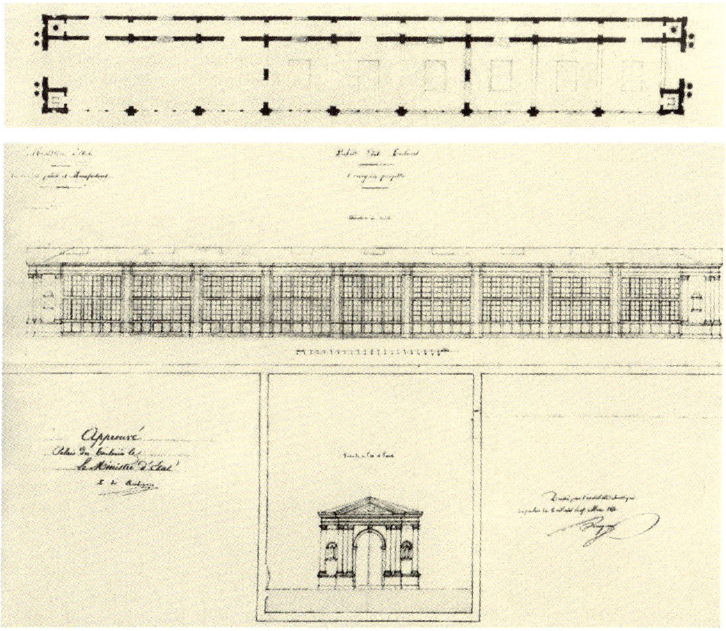

Drawings of 15 March 1852 for the Orangerie des Tuileries, by Firmin Bourgeois: plan and elevation of the south side and west front

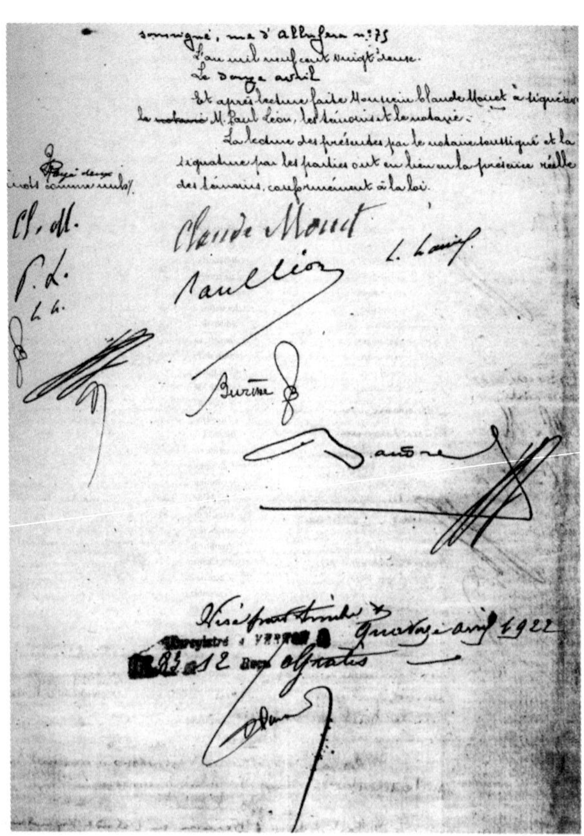

L'an mil neuf cent vingt-deux
Le douze avril

Claude Monet
Paul Léon

End page of the deed drawn up for the donation of the *Water-lilies*, 12 April 1922. Beneath Monet's signature is that of the director of the Beaux-Arts, Paul Léon, on behalf of the French State

Right-hand page: Final state of the refurbishment of the Orangerie, by Camille Lefèvre, 1927 (plan and south elevation)

Clemenceau being greeted by officials at the Orangerie on the eve of the opening of the *Water-lilies*, March 1927

The Orangerie was not an obvious choice to house the *Water-lilies* and the ensuing refurbishment proved to be a lengthy process. As early as 1897, Monet had broadly sketched out his project, but on a small scale and with no particular location for it in mind. When he set about completing the series seventeen years later it was still without a location. He worked full tilt right through the four war years painting 'panel' upon 'panel' and doubling their height. Did he already have in mind a public art project? Only in the wake of the armistice, when France was in a state of great emotional upheaval, did he decide, spurred on by Clemenceau, to make the historic gesture that would fully justify the enterprise. The only recipient of commensurate magnitude was the French nation itself, and beyond lay an unknown public of the future. Now it only remained to make it happen. Alongside his creative misgivings and anguish ('a true artist is never satisfied,' Clemenceau wrote to him affectionately, warning him against the temptation to turn out a 'super masterpiece'), Monet had to contend with officialdom, work with an architect – and find a suitable location.

L'ORANGERIE DES TVILERIES
LONGITVDINALE

c. 1860

c. 1930

c. 1970

2006

An 'oasis' of *Water-lilies*

'We fancy keeping it on the walls just as it is, hanging in hushed rooms where passers-by may seek distraction from the burdens of living in society, ease their weariness and bask in a love of nature in all its boundlessness.' Penned in 1909 after the opening of Monet's 'Waterscapes' exhibition, these lines of Gustave Geffroy could be seen as prophetic but for the fact that they were obviously inspired by Monet himself. That quasi-therapeutic experience they conjure up was what visitors encountered from the very day the Orangerie opened in 1927. It was what a man alienated from society, or more precisely, from the cramped and artificial life of the city, would have experienced. This communing with nature to which the *Water-lilies* invite the spectator thus acquires significance right at the heart of the city. Outside on the doorstep there is the Place de la Concorde, that archetypal urban setting, pure product of the classicists' geometric ideal and frenetic crossroads of modern Paris.

Monet takes viewers on that same journey that led him from the city – and from a nature warped by urban ways – towards an eternal commingling of primordial elements. He steers them away from history's turmoil towards a vital reality from which they have been cut off. Transgressing the implicit code that wrapped public art in scholarly discourse and characterless form, he exalts the very values that negate it. 'Living in society', the vindication of work and progress, together with national history: such was the subject matter of Republican public art almost to the exclusion of anything else. Monet, however, displayed on the walls of the Orangerie painting that broke with all conventions. It is 'pure' painting, albeit continuing to assert its imitative function, but of such freedom of expression that nearly a hundred years of modern art have not been enough to exhaust its lessons.

Monet's 'water garden' at Giverny, model for the *Water-lilies*, photographed by Etienne Clémentel

Detail of *Les Deux Saules*, room 2, Musée de l'Orangerie

No land in sight, a few tree-trunks emerging from the
here the mind roams in rapture, as though

water, no skies, beyond those reflected in gleaming ripples;
transported to a kingdom of tinted harmonies …

Two big oval rooms run alongside the Seine, in a cleverly tied double bow, preceded by a lobby, also oval in shape but smaller and of different orientation. Nothing but sweeping curves, ellipses quietly echoed in the pattern of the paving; bare surfaces, almost void of mouldings, fashioned merely as a backdrop to the watery décor … all that conveys a sense of gliding, an attenuated fluidity that lends itself marvellously to these unhurried surroundings, to this spot where daydreams waft by.

Louis Gillet, 1927

Splendours and miseries

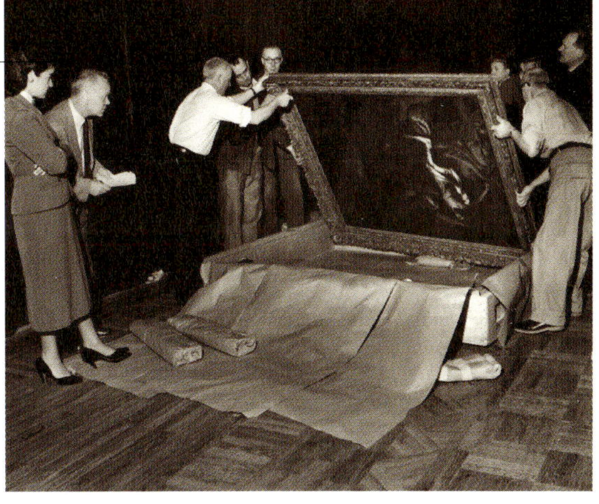

Setting up the exhibition 'From David to Toulouse-Lautrec: masterpieces from American collections' (poster, below left), held at the Musée de l'Orangerie from 20 April to 30 July 1959: unpacking *La Mise au tombeau* by Eugène Delacroix

As the *Water-lilies* only took up the eastern half of the building, the other half was turned into a sequence of rooms available for national museums to mount exhibitions. Over a span of thirty years, from 1929 to 1959, the rooms served as venue for around a hundred shows, some of which were to leave a lasting mark on the history of taste. Moreover, during all those years the *Water-lilies* had fallen out of favour and people seldom went to the Orangerie to see anything but the temporary shows. However, an event took place that was to give permanent shape to the museum's holdings: the acquisition of the Jean Walter and Paul Guillaume Collection in 1959 and 1963. Yet the arrival of this outstanding group of pictures went hand in hand with a disastrous reorganization of the space: the *Water-lilies* were sidelined, the setting Monet had created for them devastated and the collection itself was given an installation that was both pretentious and cramped. Bereft of space and funding, and falling into disrepair, the Orangerie nevertheless maintained its popularity, through the exhibitions held there until 1979, and afterwards by virtue of its permanent collections alone, with attendance figures rising from 218,422 in 1984 to 503,147 in 1998!

Le Ministre de l'Education Nationale vous prie de lui faire l'honneur d'assister le samedi 24 novembre 1934, à 15 heures, à l'inauguration de l'Exposition des

PEINTRES DE LA RÉALITÉ
EN FRANCE
AU XVIIe SIÈCLE

à l'Orangerie des Tuileries.

ENTRÉE VALABLE
POUR 2 PERSONNES

Left, the terrace of the Orangerie in 1955; above, invitation card to the legendary 1934 exhibition 'Painters of Reality in France in the 17th century' that led to a widespread revival of interest in art of this period.

1937: 'Degas' exhibition. **1942**: Under German occupation, opening of the retrospective of the official sculptor of the Third Reich, Arno Brecker. **1946**: Setting up the exhibition 'Masterpieces from French collections found in Germany by the Art Recovery Commission and the Allies'. **1955**: Exhibition 'From David to Toulouse-Lautrec'. **1959**: André Malraux at the exhibition 'Art of the Champagne region in the Middle Ages'. **1971**: Max Ernst showing Jacques Duhamel round his retrospective. **1972**: Georges de La Tour exhibition

Refurbishing the Orangerie to accommodate the Jean Walter and Paul Guillaume Collection – in which Domenica Walter, widow and heir of Paul Guillaume held a beneficial interest until her death in 1977 – was no easy task for the architect, Olivier Lahalle. He had to find room within a crammed building and yield to the various and vacillating exigencies of the domineering Domenica. Along the whole length of what was still a single-storey building a new floor was added between 1960 and 1965 to house the collection once it was permanently accessioned (and until such time, to provide temporary exhibition space). Intending to evoke 'a private residence with classical overtones', Domenica insisted upon a dreary series of rooms that did little for the dynamics of the collection, preceded by a monumental staircase with wrought-iron balustrade by Raymond Subes. All that was left of the building's earlier state was the double ellipse of the *Water-lilies*. But the building work was entirely carried out to the detriment of the latter and their treatment (about which nobody then seemed to worry) was a bundle of contradictions. Unbelievably, installing the new floor entailed blocking natural light from Monet's work, and even the handsome lobby that had been its *pronaos* was walled up and remodelled. As for the exterior, it was simply neglected.

Top: The main staircase by Olivier Lahalle and Raymond Subes, photographed by Martine Franck in 1970. Bottom, from left to right: The lobby for the *Water-lilies* in its original state …

… Here there is another Pilgrimage, departing not
but setting forth across mysterious waters, tremb

to an Isle of Cythera close by and within grasp,
ling and unfathomable. André Dezarrois, 1927

List of illustrations

The Musée de l'Orangerie was refurbished by the Agence Brochet-Lajus-Pueyo.

Unless otherwise stated, the works illustrated belong to the Jean Walter and Paul Guillaume Collection at the Musée de l'Orangerie.

'The only one of its kind'
Detail showing the south elevation of the Musée de l'Orangerie, 2006. Photo M. Chassat.
Claude Monet, *Les Tuileries, étude*, 1875, oil on canvas, 19 5/8 x 29 1/2 in. (50 x 75 cm). Musée d'Orsay, Paris. Photo RMN/Hervé Lewandowski.
Models of the four successive states of the Orangerie, made by Artefact, Paris, 2006. Photos RMN/Hervé Lewandowski.

From orangery to museum
Exhibition of the Société Centrale d'Horticulture held at the Orangerie des Tuileries, 1878. Bibliothèque Nationale de France, Paris. Photo BnF.
Project of 15 March 1852 for the Orangerie des Tuileries, by Firmin Bourgeois, plan and south and west elevations. Archives Nationales, Paris. Photo *idem.*
Posters for a dog show held on the waterside terrace and for an exhibition of painters and sculptors of hunting and shooting scenes, held inside the Orangerie, 1906. Photo Kharbine-Tapabor.
The Orangerie des Tuileries, seen from the waterside terrace, c. 1900. Photo ND/Roger-Viollet.
Double-page spread
End page of the deed drawn up for the donation of the *Water-lilies*, 12 April 1922. Photo DR.
Georges Clemenceau being greeted at the Orangerie on the eve of the official opening of the *Water-lilies*, May 1927. Photo DR.
Final state of the refurbishment of the Orangerie, by Camille Lefèvre, 1927, plan and south elevation. Archives Nationales, Paris. Photo *idem.*
Room 2 of the *Water-lilies* in its original state, 1927. Photo Monum.

An 'oasis' of *Water-lilies*
Monet's 'water garden' at Giverny, model for the *Water-lilies*, photographed by Étienne Clémentel between 1915 and 1924. Musée d'Orsay, Paris. Photo RMN/Rights reserved.
Detail of *Les Deux Saules*, room 2 of the *Water-lilies.* Photo RMN/Hervé Lewandowski.
Double-page spread
Room 1 of the *Water-lilies*, 2006. Photo Gallimard/Patrick Léger.
Reflets verts, east panel in room 1 of the *Water-lilies*, 2006. Photo *idem.*
Room 2 of the *Water-lilies*, 2006. Photo *idem.*
Reflets d'arbres, west panel in room 2 of the *Water-lilies*, 2006. Photo *idem.*

Splendours and miseries
Setting up the exhibition 'From David to Toulouse-Lautrec: masterpieces from American collections', held at the Musée de l'Orangerie from 20 April to 30 July 1959: unpacking *La Mise au tombeau* by Delacroix. Photo Keystone/Hachette Photos.
Poster for the exhibition 'From David to Toulouse-Lautrec: masterpieces from American collections', on the Orangerie terrace in 1955. Photo Keystone/Hachette Photos.
Invitation card to the exhibition 'Painters of reality in France in the 17th Century', 1934. Musée de l'Orangerie archives. Photo *idem.*
The exhibition 'L'Art de Versailles', 1932, pastel by Léopold Delbeke. Musée d'Orsay, Paris. Photo RMN/Hervé Lewandowski.
Poster of the 'David' exhibition held at the Orangerie des Tuileries from 24 June to 30 October 1948. Photo Kharbine-Tapabor.
Poster of the exhibition 'Van Gogh and the painters of Auvers-sur-Oise', held at the Orangerie des Tuileries from 26 November 1954 to 28 February 1955. Photo Kharbine-Tapabor.
Poster of the exhibition 'Monet, the *Water-lilies* cycle', held at the Musée de l'Orangerie from 6 May to 2 August 1999. Musée de l'Orangerie archives.
Double-page spread.
Under German occupation, opening of the retrospective of the official sculptor of the Third Reich, Arno Brecker, held at the Orangerie des Tuileries from 2 to 31 August 1942. Photo Keystone/Hachette Photos.
Visitors to the 'Degas' exhibition, held at the Orangerie des Tuileries from 6 March to 3 May 1937. Photo Keystone/Hachette Photos.
Setting up the exhibition 'Masterpieces from French collections found in Germany by the Art Recovery Commission and the Allies', held at the Orangerie des Tuileries from 12 June to 3 November 1946. Photo Keystone/Hachette Photos.
Visitors to the exhibition 'From David to Toulouse-Lautrec: masterpieces from American collections', held at the Orangerie from 20 April to 30 July 1959. Photo Keystone/Hachette Photos.
André Malraux at the exhibition 'Art of the Champagne region in the Middle Ages', held at the Orangerie des Tuileries from 15 April to 17 July 1959. Photo Keystone/Hachette Photos.
Max Ernst showing Jacques Duhamel round his retrospective held at the Orangerie des Tuileries in April 1971. Photo Keystone/Hachette Photos.
View of one of the rooms at the exhibition 'Georges de La Tour', held at the Musée de l'Orangerie in 1972.
The main staircase by Olivier Lahalle and Raymond Subes, photographed by Martine Franck, 1970. Photo Magnum/Martine Franck.
The lobby leading to the *Water-lilies*, on the left in its original state and on the right after 'renovation' in the 1960-65 project. Photos Musée de l'Orangerie archives.
Visitors in the Derain room of the Musée de l'Orangerie in 1994. Photo Musée de l'Orangerie archives.
North elevation of the Musée de l'Orangerie, Tuileries Gardens side, in 1990. Photo Musée de l'Orangerie archives.
Major phases in the building works, 2000-6, photographed by Jean-Christophe Ballot. © Jean-Christophe Ballot.

An open-minded approach
Paul Cézanne, *La Barque et les baigneurs*, c. 1890, oil on canvas, 36 1/4 x 49 1/4 in. (92 x 125 cm). Photo RMN/Hervé Lewandowski.
André Derain, *Portrait de Paul Guillaume*, c. 1919-20, oil on canvas, 31 7/8 x 25 in. (81 x 64 cm). Photo RMN/Christian Jean. © ADAGP, Paris, 2006.
Chaïm Soutine, *Le Petit Pâtissier*, c. 1922-23, oil on canvas, 28 3/4 x 21 1/4 in. (73 x 54 cm). Photo RMN/Thierry Le Mage. © ADAGP, Paris, 2006.
Amedeo Modigliani, *Fille rousse*, 1915, oil on canvas, 16 x 14 3/8 in. (40.5 x 36.5 cm). Photo RMN/Thierry Le Mage.
Marie Laurencin, *Les Biches*, 1923, oil on canvas, 28 3/4 x 36 1/4 in. (73 x 92 cm). Photo RMN/Hervé Lewandowski. © ADAGP, Paris, 2006.

The thinking behind it

The success of the renovation of the Orangerie depended on a number of factors, in particular an ability to identify the key issues and to evaluate the divergence of aims and accomplishments, values and practices between the 1920s and the turn of the century, a period that saw the *Water-lilies* pass from neglect to triumph, modern art achieve gradual acceptance following its difficult breakthrough, and the rise of the current museum mania. With all that in mind, it was possible to sketch out the ends and means of renewal.

Guiding principles

Ends did indeed come before means. There was inevitably a range of practical measures to be addressed – such as restoring the dilapidated façades and roof, increasing the surface area, improving the facilities and easing congestion, tackling the lighting, and climatic and working conditions. But the most important consideration was to put the Orangerie back into the limelight, bringing to the fore the things that make it so special. That in fact was the thinking behind it. For the *Water-lilies* as well as for the Jean Walter and Paul Guillaume Collection, the challenge was to find a way to express their inherent qualities and heighten their affinities. At the same time it was to highlight the harmony existing between this duo and the music of the site; and to make a feature of the building's 'character' which Monet had perceived and so superbly integrated to his purpose, but which had been lost through successive refurbishments. These few guiding principles were the starting point for a study plan that would precede the architectural project itself.

It was intended to recapture the spirit not the letter and thus transcend an 'archaeological' process that would have resulted in tying the Orangerie to outmoded and altogether minor arrangements. So the idea of replicating the interior of Paul Guillaume's apartment was discarded (in the first instance that was impossible, since too many things had changed in the make-up of the collection). Reverting to the original décor of the lobby and the floors in the *Water-lilies* rooms according to the norms of museum architecture of the period was likewise rejected.

It was also intended to embrace wholeheartedly those little-known attributes seen to be at risk which, though a 'small museum', make the Orangerie irreplaceable. For Monet's paintings they were the absolute primacy of contemplation and delight, lying at the core of his objectives and a vital ingredient of the aesthetic experience. For the Collection they were its myriad precious tones and accents, but above all its predominantly classical aspect, running counter to the accepted image but not to the reality of modern art, and especially important to promote as modern art had begun to question its own inhibited attitude. All that was to happen without losing sight of the noble educational mission of a State museum, so long as that was tailored to the very specific aims of this museum, rather than drifting into the muddle of some sweeping 'cultural action'.

As a consequence of this approach, well-grounded in reasoned (but ardent) appreciation of the specific nature of the place and of the works, the acquisition of extra space and the drawing up of a general plan would be carried out with due respect for the historical structure of the Orangerie. The same held true for those priorities dictated by its contents, namely supremacy of the highly significant east-west axis, human scale, contemplation and scrutiny. Nevertheless, while being expected to make assertive choices and display a clear inventiveness, the architect-to-be would do so at the exclusive service of the works and the thinking behind their presentation. In that respect, the project broke decisively with that architectural ostentation found in museums in the 1970s and 80s, which was practised at the expense of famed works of art and was at times a substitute for studied reflection.

For the *Water-lilies*, whose purpose had lost none of its relevance and so clearly derived from the arrangement conceived by Monet, it was simply a matter of reverting to that purpose – in so far as that was possible! The lobby, which had been destroyed, needed rebuilding and numerous entrances, which had formerly allowed a free flow of traffic, had to be reopened. The hideous square-panelled ceiling had to be replaced with awnings and a radical remedy found for the labyrinthine nature of the tour by creating direct step-free access from the museum entrance to Monet's work. At long last the *Water-lilies* would become the living heart of the museum. Visitors approaching the Orangerie via the terrace (or via the ramp linking it to the gardens) would proceed smoothly, without changing levels, from the bustle of the city to a grand continuum where they would immerse themselves in silence and beauty.

The same urge to restore full meaning to the collections was to apply also to the Jean Walter and Paul Guillaume Collection. Hitherto, in spite of its splendour, it had seemingly only offered a somewhat incomplete survey of painting from Impressionism to the 1920s, without much raison d'être when put alongside Beaubourg or the Musée d'Orsay. It had now to be demonstrated that here indeed was an important selection, fruit of the discriminating taste of a great connoisseur and of the open-mindedness of an unbiased observer. It was planned to tackle the 'historical' dimension of the Collection by means of a documentary introduction presenting the personality and work of the collector: an intensive research campaign and the providential gift of a private archive were to make this possible. The aesthetic identity of the assemblage depended on how the pictures were hung and how their contrasts and affinities were given due prominence.

Finally the architect was to highlight the unity of the architectural setting, the vehicle and symbol of the museum's own unity, as well as its relationship with the city (its antithesis) and with the landscaping of water and greenery that shared a kinship with the *Water-lilies*.

But if this was the thinking behind it, the works and the space had nevertheless to be allowed to speak for themselves, since a museum is neither a book nor a school. This was particularly true of the Orangerie, whose founding fathers intended that it should communicate only through the language of forms and speak much more to the senses than to the intellect. In the refurbished Orangerie information and written commentary would thus be used sparingly. Likewise, publishing and educational activities (conferences, screenings and exhibitions in keeping with the scale of the location) would be restricted to helping visitors extend their knowledge of the museum.

A discreet masterwork

This then was the canvas which set the parameters of the architect's brief, but which left him creative scope. The Orangerie was fortunate to find in Olivier Brochet's talent that exceptional blend of discretion and determination needed to give shape to the project without betraying its purpose. Sound and yet sure-footed, at once daring and refined, his architectural project, selected in 1998 following an open competition, was to be the way forward to fruition.

Underneath this success lay a stroke of genius. There were countless practical difficulties that hindered this major restructuring; the most obvious was also the toughest: the lack of space. Outside, no extension seemed possible, the building being listed as an historical monument. Inside, it hardly seemed possible either: the 1960s storey, where the Jean Walter and Paul Guillaume Collection was already tightly squeezed in, precluded the acquisition of any more space upwards. Only in the western half was it possible to gain more space downwards. The other half sheltered the delicate *Water-lilies*, which were stuck immovably to the walls, thereby precluding any digging in that area. Moreover, any attempt at mere redeployment of the existing space ran into problems of sheer saturation. Clearing at the very most 5,350 square feet of windowless basement would hardly have been enough to house the service departments. How could provision be made for a public area big enough to cope with the number of visitors;

how could a bookshop, educational facilities, and temporary exhibition spaces, even limited ones, be accommodated? How could openings to the outside be made? How, above all, could the original lobby for the *Water-lilies* be re-created and breathing space given to the Collection with room for a documentary introduction? There was also the crucial problem of lighting the *Water-lilies:* how could daylight be brought back to them without compromising the Collection overhead? The study plan recommended the removal of the grand staircase leading to the upper floor, but did not go as far as demolishing the floor itself. The architect boldly supplied an unexpected solution. He proposed not only digging under the western half of the building, but also under the lawn flanking the museum on the garden side. Then, in this new underground space, the exhibition rooms and part of the services could be installed. Last but not least, the Collection could also be moved there, into spaces directly accessible from the main entrance and partially lit with natural light through fenestration running along the north wall. This way the missing square footage had been found. The additions of the 1960s could be knocked down and the old building restructured at will – everything but the walls and the floor of the rooms housing the *Water-lilies.* And they would see living daylight again. Cutting them off from natural light had been the worst outrage inflicted upon them in their years of neglect.

Financing had still to be provided, since the cost of the whole undertaking, albeit modest, exceeded the funding that the Ministère de la Culture was willing to invest. The museum took it upon itself to generate funds by putting on the road an international travelling exhibition of highlights from the Collection, which flew the flag of the Orangerie around the world. This show was seen by more than three million visitors and paid a sizeable share of the building costs. It was now possible for the long-mooted but as yet unrealised project to receive the expert and faithful translation as proposed by Olivier Brochet.

The architect was in fact to tackle with utmost aplomb and intellectual rigour the architectural problems of the museum, resulting in a perfect functional layout with the freest circulation possible, all the while adhering to the 'philosophy' behind the project.

The changing circumstances in the course of construction only slightly affected these distinctive features. White and grey, in turn solid and crystalline, the sober architecture of stone, stucco and bare concrete, in the constructivist and purist vein exemplified by Le Corbusier, submits loyally to the supremacy of the works of art, isolating them from the unhallowed space outside and enveloping them in a climate of contemplation. There is an understated monumentality, which befits the dignity of the place and magnifies its intellectual axes. This is apparent in the rectilinear opening to the lower gallery, in the two giant conical skylights pouring light onto the *Water-lilies* (they can be glimpsed through the canopies), in the reception and orientation area occupying to full height the western half of the old orangery, where exposed beams and pilasters are a reminder of the original roof truss. Bathed in light through two long glazed façades, this space is the fulcrum of the museum and a magical meeting point of elements. To the north and south are the gardens, the Seine, and Paris, so near and yet so far. To the west is the concrete block of the administrative offices. To the east, in a special view, rises a high wall screening off the *Water-lilies*; and before it, crossed by a gently rising footbridge leading towards them, a broad staircase goes down to the Jean Walter and Paul Guillaume Collection and the exhibition area. All told, it is a masterly arrangement whose simplicity belies its ingenuity.

On the other hand, the architect's intervention in those spaces directly devoted to the collections has been minimal. For the *Water-lilies*, other than their 'sun-blinds', he only worked on the lobby, replacing the old polychrome floor with a light grey one and erecting the all-white walls. For the Jean Walter and Paul Guillaume Collection, he installed elegant windows and created a pleasing view with the two-roomed historical overture based on a concept of the museum's director.

All in all, there is nothing gratuitous or injudicious about this architectural discourse, which has an understated eloquence. Olivier Brochet's work is laudable and will receive accolades for its brilliant know-how, as well as for its austere and serene beauty. There is nothing about it that is not in harmony with the identity and vocation of the Orangerie: it has supremacy of judgement, a human scale and unity of place, blending with the site without at all upsetting its contemplative tonality. In short, everything was undertaken with due consideration and love for great works of art.

Installing the collections remained to be done – or more accurately, installing the Jean Walter and Paul Guillaume Collection, since for the *Water-lilies* installation it was more a matter of going back to its origins. The pictures fitted perfectly into the spaces, which had been tailor-made for them. By way of preamble, the Paul Guillaume room and its counterpart, the so-called Interiors Room, tell the story of how the Collection came about and acquaint visitors with the collector. The first does this through a selection of archival items and original works – notably some African sculptures that belonged to Paul Guillaume and have been loaned by the Musée du Quai Branly. The second shows views of interiors at the Guillaume's apartment in the Avenue Foch through splendid miniature models. It also features a life-size re-creation of a corner of Domenica's library in the Rue du Cirque, complete with furniture and paintings. Then comes the Collection itself. While remaining logical, the layout and

The 'frontispiece' to the *Water-lilies*, as planned (above) and as built (right)

installation attempt to bring out the Collection's diversity – the ardour of Soutine and the 'naivety' of Rousseau contrasting with the majesty of 'modern classicism' – and its cohesiveness – Picasso, Matisse and Derain following on from Cézanne and Renoir, with Cubism in harmony with the refined Realism of the 1920s.

In addition, preceding the *Water-lilies* and scattered around the Collection are a series of information panels. Along with documentary films shown uninterruptedly in the audio-visual room, they provide visitors with historical data and brief artistic analysis. On the landing of the main stairs further panels give a short history of the museum and the building, of which four models show successive 'states'. Nearby there is a bust of Clemenceau, the energetic champion

of the *Water-lilies*, without whom the Orangerie would not be what it is. Lastly, on the same axis as the stairs, Derain's large painting *L'Âge d'or*, on loan from the Musée National d'Art Moderne, provides both a physical and metaphoric link between the two levels of the tour. This picture echoes the *Water-lilies* in format and range of colours, providing a fitting prelude to the Collection, of which Derain is one of the highlights.

Last hurdles

A few words more ought to be said about two occurrences in the course of construction works that affected the nature of the project and left their mark. The first severely disrupted the scheduling. Hardly had the mechanical diggers begun working on the underground extension – after an archaeological appraiser's report had concluded that there were no remains – than they struck the remnants of an old

16th-century city wall. Thought to have been pulled down at the time of the terrace's construction in the following century, its discovery caused something of a stir and petitions were signed to preserve the wall in its entirety. But these remnants cut diagonally across the building site and were thus completely out of line with the dominant axis and the *Water-lilies* – indeed of the new plan as a whole. An expert board of enquiry was called in to resolve this conflict of interests. It recommended creating a small room devoted to the history of the wall and how it was built. The room would be located away from the other spaces, in an area on the south side of the basement of the historic building where the remains were most complete. A sample length of about twenty-five feet would be preserved, thought to be a long enough section since a huge block of the same wall can be seen in the Place de la Concorde, where it serves to bolster the terrace. This recommendation, supported by the architect and the museum, was nevertheless rejected. Only after countless public statements and reversals of opinion was it decided to truncate the temporary exhibition space and two other rooms in order to re-erect on the north side a section stretching to almost fifty feet. As they could not be seen from the gallery, this at least had the virtue of preserving the impact of the east-west axis.

Something else unforeseen arose, this time independent of all external pressure. On the way into the *Water-lilies*, right below the grand staircase, the architect had envisaged a great white wall, a veritable 'frontispiece' to this secular sanctuary. It would have marked the transition from real unhallowed space – namely the entrance hall, with its walls of squared bare concrete – to a space of dreams and timelessness. A decision at an advanced stage from on high left no option but to replace it with a wall identical to the others.

In spite of these hurdles, those who have brought renewal to the Orangerie feel they have, broadly speaking, attained their goal. What does the future hold? Will it be possible to preserve such a delicate identity, which took so long to acquire? Will this place imbued with meaning be able to escape trivialization? Will this offering of two distinguished souls resist commercialization? We should like to hope so.

English Bibliography

Michel Hoog, *Musée de l'Orangerie, les Nymphéas of Claude Monet*, RMN, 1989 (reprinted in 2006)

Michel Hoog, *Musée de l'Orangerie, Catalogue of the Jean Walter and Paul Guillaume Collection*, RMN, 1987

French Bibliography

In the same series as this book:

Pierre Georgel, *Les Nymphéas*, Gallimard/RMN, 2006

Pierre Georgel, *La Collection Jean Walter et Paul Guillaume* , Gallimard/RMN, 2006

Pierre Georgel, *Le musée de l'Orangerie*, Gallimard/RMN, 2006

Permanent educational displays and temporary exhibitions illustrate and expand on the museum's original purpose. And the public, who already flocked there in the years of neglect, has at last been accorded a quality of reception that matches its enthusiasm.

The visitor's route speaks for itself: facing you are the *Water-lilies* aligned along the royal axis, which Monet followed to hang his paintings (reached before 1960 from the north side, and then, until 1999, by means of a maze of stairs). Then, downstairs you can see the Jean Walter and Paul Guillaume Collection as well as temporary exhibitions. The lobby, which was originally an integral part of the display of the *Water-lilies*, is back and now refined (below left). As before, the paintings are lit by daylight filtered through awnings (below right). A rugged mass of raw concrete providing office space faces their watery and airy dream.

Ground-floor plan

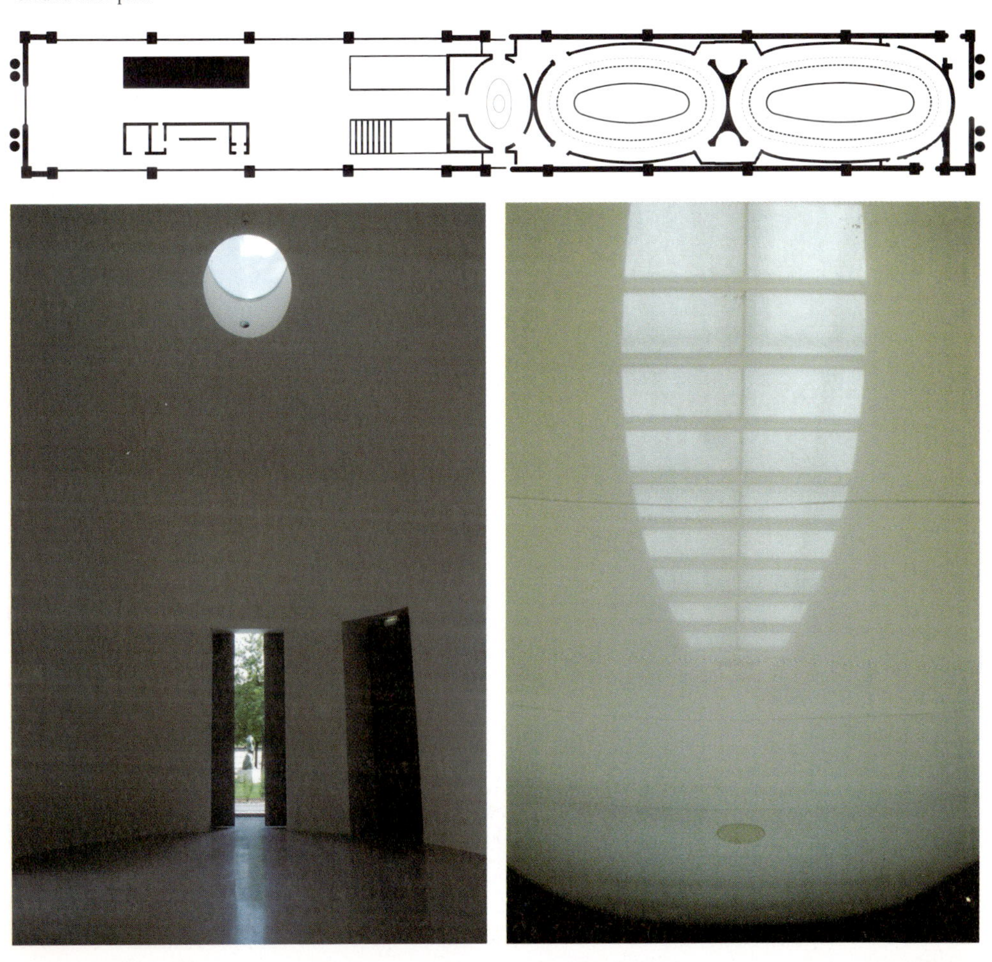

At the end of the tour, there is a short length of restored stone facing from an old Paris city wall. Built in the 16th century, then pulled down, it had been partially preserved under the terrace where the orangery was to be erected. Another fragment may be seen outside, on the west side of the terrace by the Place de la Concorde.

Paris has rediscovered a museum on a human scale.
It shimmers with the lights of the city.
And, more than any other, it exudes delight.
Nicole Duault, *Le Journal du dimanche*, 7 May 2006

1• *L'Âge d'or* by Derain
2• Paul Guillaume room
3• Interiors room
4• Tutelary figures: Cézanne and Renoir
5• Modern classicism: Matisse / Picasso / Derain
6• 'Modern primitives': Rousseau / Modigliani / Laurencin
7• Torments and bursts: Utrillo / Soutine

André Derain, *Paysage du Midi*, c. 1932, oil on canvas

Classics of the 20th century

Having been modified by Domenica in accordance with her tastes of a distinctly more traditional bent than Paul's, the collection had a dominant classical aspect by the time it reached the Orangerie, thereby making it beyond all doubt the most representative public assemblage of 'modern classicism'. This trend within modern art, for a long time hidden from view by the hegemony of the avant-garde, won almost uninterrupted acclaim from the 1880s to the 1930s. It is defined by a tempered adherence to the visible, by a steadfast desire for order and harmony (but with an irrational hint of eeriness) and for the timeless beauty incarnate in the human, especially female, body. In short, it embodied a continuation or a resurgence of values which, although rejected by the aesthetic revolutions of the 20th century, remained objects of nostalgia. Hence there were frequent allusions to the 'masters', to sculptors of Greco-Roman antiquity, to revered figures in the 'grand tradition' like Raphael, Poussin or Corot, but also to Cézanne and Renoir, who with their blend of classical continuity and modern innovations served as privileged models around 1920-25.

The leaders of modernism, Picasso, Matisse and Derain were also rather surprisingly the protagonists of a classicizing tendency that appeared to be the opposite. In Picasso's work, the human figure's supremacy of form and prestige preceded their fragmentation in the Cubist experiment and then made a magisterial comeback with the 'giant women' of the 1920s.

Pablo Picasso, *Grand nu à la draperie*, 1920-21, oil on canvas

Our youthfulness antique,
Pale flesh and darkling form,
Takes pride in the mystique
That is of numbers born!

Girls of golden numbers,
With heaven's laws imbued;
On us falls and slumbers
A god all honey-hued.

Paul Valéry, 1922

Pablo Picasso, *Femme au peigne*, 1906, gouache on paper mounted on linen

Any classical programme is fallacious if it boasts an ontological or social foundation; or even simply calls to witness values that may already have been determined and decreed to be the truth. But if it abides by a sensitivity to form, to impressions of harmony, to the experience of beauty – which for some has as much supremacy as beholding Etna at night – that, on the other hand, does ring true, since it reinstates the human project at its best capacity.

Yves Bonnefoy, 1996

Henri Matisse,, *Odalisque à la culotte grise*, 1927, oil on canvas

André Derain, *Nu à la cruche*, c. 1925, oil on canvas

In a space between the gallery and the inner rooms two nudes – one by Renoir and one by Derain – have been juxtaposed; revealing the interplay of affiliations within 'modern classicism'.

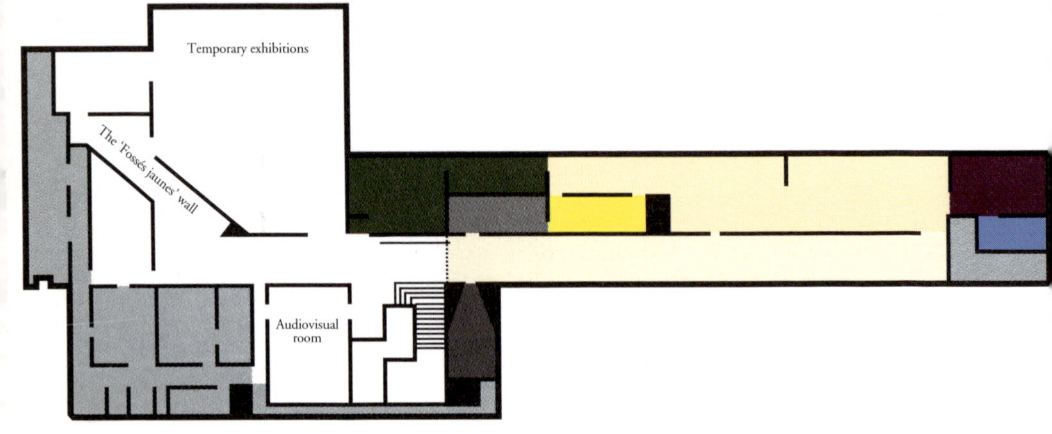

On the landing of the central staircase, architects' models and a bust of Clemenceau by Rodin illustrate the history of the Orangerie. Downstairs, a large canvas by Derain, *L'Âge d'or*, on loan from the Centre Pompidou, marks the entrance to the Jean Walter and Paul Guillaume Collection, the story of which is told in two small rooms. Then comes a long bright walkway – a gallery (in the tradition of receding perspective and evenly spaced columns) – and in two large rooms branching off it, presenting the continuum

of 'modern classicism', from Renoir and Cézanne to Matisse and Derain, with Picasso serving as a common denominator. Two other suites of rooms, with their walls painted in distinctive hues contrasting with the first ones, display aspects of modern art that are more familiar to the public. The first of these centres on the theme of primitivism with works by Rousseau, Modigliani and Laurencin on display, and the second on Expressionism, with Utrillo and – honour to whom honour is due – Soutine, whose dazzling works light up the end of the tour. But within this highly structured layout, the groupings are very informal, inspired by the thoroughly intuitive approach of the collector, who was aware of unobserved and at times astonishingly revealing affinities. So, Modigliani, often linked to Soutine on the grounds of their friendship, is here 'wedded' to Rousseau, whose round faces and squat bodies echo those of his *Antonia*, and to Laurencin, whose delicate palette and flowing outlines evoke those of the *Jeune Apprenti* or the *Femme au ruban de velours*.

Back to its origins

After a period of construction that had been something of an obstacle course, the Orangerie was reopened to the public in the spring of 2006. Rethought and restructured, it is the antithesis of the way it was before. It has been opened up to natural light, which bathes the *Water-lilies* anew and also to the surrounding gardens, which are drawn into the lobby area through the vast glazed bays. The route for visitors is clear and serene and the sparing décor inspires contemplation. Both the *Water-lilies* and the Jean Walter and Paul Guillaume Collection now have room to breathe and function smoothly and distinctly, each group asserting its own identity. The location itself reveals its long-hidden structure and the contrasting milestones of its history. With its architecture that eschews the archaic, the museum has returned to its origins, taking up its founding fathers' philosophy that time has not tarnished; it has even acquired the unity that was lacking.

What variety and yet what unison are there in this collection! Soutine's fervour sits cheek by jowl with the gracefulness of Renoir and Laurencin, while the composure of Utrillo's *Notre-Dame* or Douanier Rousseau's *La Noce* harmonizes with that of Cézanne's portraits, as it does with the frontality of Modigliani's portrait of 1915! However, when first put on show in 1966, this delicately poised symphony turned the custodians of the modernist flame into arbiters of taste. 'Paul Guillaume,' thus opined the female Paris correspondent for *Art News*, 'opted oftener for the delicate or the sentimental than for

invention in its more brutal phases.' Since the 'brutality' of invention, in other words its radical and violent nature, had become the sole criterion for a modern work, almost all the collection was discredited!

Above: Chaïm Soutine, *Le Petit Pâtissier*, c. 1922-23, oil on canvas; right: Marie Laurencin, *Les Biches*, 1923, oil on canvas
Far right: Amedeo Modigliani, *Fille rousse*, 1915, oil on canvas; left-hand page: André Derain, *Portrait de Paul Guillaume*, c. 1919-20, oil on canvas

Henri Rousseau, known as Le Douanier Rousseau, *La Noce*, c. 1905, oil on canvas

aurice Utrillo, *Notre-Dame*, c. 1910, oil on canvas

Henri Matisse, *Le Boudoir*, 1921, oil on canvas

Pablo Picasso, *L'Étreinte*,
1903, pastel

An open-minded approach

Paul Cézanne, *La Barque et les baigneurs*, c. 1888, oil on canvas

The Jean Walter and Paul Guillaume Collection was amassed between the First World War and the 1930s by a young picture dealer, Paul Guillaume (1891-1934), who, despairing of the authorities ever doing anything about it, envisioned creating his own museum to give 'the true measure of living art in the world'. Expanded and markedly transformed by Paul's widow, Domenica (Madame Jean Walter by her second marriage), the collection reflects the taste at once exacting and liberal of its founder. A resolute advocate of modern art, Paul Guillaume was concerned before all else about excellence and convinced that tradition and modernity were not mutually exclusive. Drawing from the highly diverse breeding-ground of 'living art', as well as from the most radical forms of the avant-garde (but without going as far as Surrealism or abstract art), he only partially achieved his ambitious aims. Yet thanks to the quality of his choices, and perhaps even more his extraordinary breadth of vision, the collection occupies a distinguished place among French museums today and his refusal to take a reductionist view of the avant-garde gives it a singular originality.

By now almost everything has been said about the works of art that Mme Domenica Walter has latterly brought before an admiring public. The most striking thing perhaps is that almost all of them seem to elude the criteria of modishness and style … We can but stand amazed at such sureness of taste, which has pooh-poohed passing fads and made a beeline for pictures chosen by virtue of their solidity and permanence. Jean Clair, 1966

'How,' Jean Clair wondered, 'could this man have the coolness of judgement to choose some of the most balanced Cézannes in existence and that stroke of genius of sorts that enabled him to discover and buy *L'Enfant de chœur* or *Le Garçon d'étage?* The fact remains that these paintings by Soutine … blaze like that searing splash of red on a over-cautiously executed canvas by Corot that suddenly transforms it into a masterpiece … ' As much stress was laid on the collector's independence as on his discernment.

Pierre Auguste Renoir, *Jeunes Filles au piano*, c. 1892, oil on canvas

Paul Cézanne, *Madame Cézanne au jardin*, 1879-80, oil on canvas

A half-century of prestigious exhibitions was to turn the Orangerie – along with its sister institution, the Jeu de Paume across the way, where from 1947 the Impressionist collections of the Louvre were kept – into one of Paris's great cultural focal points. Then in the late 1970s this golden age all of sudden came to an end. On the one hand, there was a new cultural focus taking shape, notably with the opening of Beaubourg, then of the Musée d'Orsay, that spelled doom for the fortunes of the Orangerie, already feeling competition from the new galleries at the Grand Palais.
On the other hand, since the collection had been bequeathed to the nation with the proviso that it was to be shown permanently and in its entirety, the whole upper floor was 'frozen' at the expiration of the usufruct on Domenica's death.
Of the 14,000 square feet or so previously devoted to exhibitions only some 3,250 were left and soon swallowed up. Almost overnight, the Orangerie had to break with its brilliant past. But in 1999 one last exhibition 'Monet: the *Water-lilies* cycle' took place, for which the building was cleared prior to its closure for major renovation (2000-6).

...e 1960-65 project. Heaps of paintings and hordes of people: the ...e north elevation in 1990. Right-hand page: A few phases in the new project.

The architect Olivier Brochet, commissioned to undertake the project devised by the museum's director (above), immediately resolved the major difficulty posed by the smallness of the building. Faced with the impossibility of increasing the surface area of the building, he devised a brilliant yet simple solution: to build an extension underground along the north side (left-hand page, below, right). It thus became possible to free up the space inside by removing the 1960-65 storey and so bring daylight back to the *Water-lilies*. The Jean Walter and Paul Guillaume Collection would be installed in the underground extension to be flooded with daylight from a long glazed gallery.

The exhibition 'L'Art de Versailles', 1932, pastel by Léopold Delbeke

Posters from three memorable exhibitions held in 1948, 1954 and 1999 respectively